I0489114

Disclaimer and Terms of Use

While all attempts have been make to verify the accuracy of information provided in this publication, neither the Author nor the Publisher assume any responsibility or liability for errors, omissions or contradictory interpretation of the subject matter presented herein. This publication is intended for general informational and educational purposes only and is not intended for use as a source of legal or financial advice. The Publisher wants to stress that the information contained herein may be subject to varying federal laws or regulations, which are subject to change. All users are advised to seek the services of competent professionals in the legal and financial fields where and when necessary, as determined by the user. The Author is not currently an employee of either the United States Government or of the Social Security Administration, nor is he currently associated with those bodies in any official or non-official capacity. The views expressed in this work are solely the personal opinions of the Author and do not necessarily represent the official views or policies of the Social Security Administration or its officials, nor does the Author have any authority to speak on their behalf.

Table of Contents

Preface

I worked as a Claims Representative in the Social Security Administration for twenty-five years. That job involved interviewing the public, both face-to-face in the office and on the phone, taking applications for benefits as well as reviewing and processing claims through SSA's computer systems to either initiate payment of benefits or issue denial notices.

Interviewing was often the most rewarding part of the job because we could see and hear expressions of appreciation from the people we were helping, and most of my interviews ended with a smile and a handshake from people who may have come into the office feeling confused, nervous or frustrated in their attempts to understand how they could apply for benefits, especially when they had been forced to leave a good job because of illness or a sudden injury. I often felt that we were, in our own way, doing God's work in helping those people, some of whom were on the brink of losing all hope before they came in.

I recently took early retirement, partly because I became increasingly frustrated that the agency, under budget constraints from Congress, had been forced to reduce staffing to the point where we could no longer give people the level of service that we were accustomed to providing. Interviewing the public became a rushed job because we had less and less employees to service the growing numbers of baby boomers filing for retirement benefits and the increasing number of people filing for disability when they could not find employment due to the Great Recession.

I felt that I was no longer allowed to do what I had been trained to do--helping people understand the benefit programs available to them--because we were too busy trying to keep up with "productivity" goals for processing applications and other workloads; quantity became more important than quality. Many of my experienced co-workers expressed similar feelings; we felt that we were being treated like assembly-line workers in a factory instead of the knowledgeable professionals that we had been trained to become.

The thought occurred to me that there must be another way to make use of all this valuable knowledge gained through experience; this book is the result. During a quarter-century of reviewing and processing disability claims, I had seen many poorly-completed applications get denied, sometimes even when the individuals filing for benefits had obvious and severe medical conditions. I have also had the personal satisfaction of seeing many applications which I had taken result in the approval of disability benefits, sometimes on the first try, and others approved after I had taken the appeal request.

I cannot promise that every person who follows the advice given here will be approved for benefits; however, I CAN promise that my advice will help you provide the medical decision-maker with the best possible case for approving your claim, thereby removing many of the stumbling blocks many applicants unknowingly place in their own path through lack of understanding of what information is actually needed.

The best general piece of advice I can give to a disability applicant is to provide the examiner with enough information that they DO need and do not waste their time with a lot of facts they don't need. It is now my job to explain the difference. Let's begin!

Introduction to Disability Benefits

You may already have some knowledge about the major types of disability programs and benefits, either from what you have heard from others or read online or in print elsewhere. Even so, you might benefit from reading this introduction because I have no way to determine how accurate or complete your knowledge is.

I hope you will forgive me if I am stating facts which may seem obvious to you because my own experience tells me that there is a vast amount of misunderstanding among the general public, which too often costs them hundreds, thousands, even tens of thousands of dollars in lost benefits just because no one ever explained what programs might be available to them; you might be shocked to hear some people admit that for years they never applied for any disability benefits because they thought Social Security was only for people of retirement age, but I have actually heard such sad stories myself.

In this section, I will provide a summary of what I believe is the minimum knowledge you need in order to understand most of the disability benefit categories and programs. It is possible that you may qualify for more than one type of benefit at the same time and should consider applying for several types of benefits simultaneously; if the benefits for which you might qualify are administered by the Social Security Administration (SSA), they are supposed to screen for possible eligibility for any and all of those categories when you apply for any one particular benefit, and they are also supposed to refer you to other agencies to apply for other programs.

First we will discuss those benefit programs administered by SSA. The two major programs which they handle are Social Security and Supplemental Security Income. Social Security provides benefits for disabled adults who have sufficient work credits on their own record, as well as childhood disability benefits for adults who qualify under a parent's record and benefits for disabled widows and widowers who qualify based upon a deceased spouse's earnings.

As you can see from the preceding sentence, "earnings" are the key factor in basic eligibility for Social Security benefits; other factors such as a qualifying relationship to the worker or even the severity of the claimant's medical condition are not considered until SSA verifies that the worker has paid in enough to the Social Security trust fund for benefits to be payable. The amount of a person's Social Security monthly benefit is based upon the worker's past earnings history.

To qualify as a childhood disability beneficiary, an adult must have become disabled prior to the age of 22 and meet Social Security's definition of being a child of a worker who is either currently entitled to Social Security benefits or is deceased. A disabled widow or widower must have become disabled between the ages of 50 and 59 and be the surviving spouse of a worker who had earned sufficient work credits by the time of death.

One point that you should keep in mind is that Social Security Disability generally does not pay for the first five months, including the month in which you became disabled, even if the medical decision is made during that period; this is known as the "waiting period," and no retroactive payments will be made after the medical decision for that period either.

Supplemental Security Income (SSI) is intended for those individuals who either do not qualify for benefits from Social Security because of insufficient earnings or whose Social Security benefit is low and whose other income and resources are not above certain limits. There are benefits for disabled individuals, blind individuals and disabled children under age 18, as well as for individuals aged 65 and over who are not necessarily disabled.

For SSI, excess income and resources are the key factors which can cause a claim to be denied regardless of the claimant's medical condition and other qualifications. There is a Federal SSI benefit payable in all 50 states, and many states also provide a state supplement, which varies from one state to another and is included with the Federal benefit in one monthly SSI payment.

A person who applies for SSI and meets the other eligibility requirements may qualify right away for up to six months of benefit payments while waiting for the medical decision if he or she has a medical condition which is defined as a presumptive disability or presumptive blindness; these conditions include the following:

1. Amputation of a leg at the hip
2. Total deafness in both ears
3. Total blindness in both eyes
4. Bed confinement and immobility without a wheelchair, walker or crutches due to a longstanding condition, excluding recent accident and recent surgery
5. Stroke (cerebral vascular accident) more than three months in the past with continued marked difficulty in walking or using a hand or arm
6. Cerebral palsy, muscular dystrophy, or muscular atrophy with marked difficulty in walking, speaking, or coordination of the hands or arms
7. Down syndrome
8. Symptomatic HIV or AIDS—Form SSA-4814 or SSA-4815 is needed (from a doctor)
9. A physician confirms by telephone or in a signed statement that an individual has a terminal illness with a life expectancy of six months or less, or a physician or knowledgeable hospice official confirms that an individual is receiving hospice services because of a terminal illness
10. Confirmation from an appropriate medical official that a spinal cord injury has produced an inability to ambulate without the use of a walker or bilateral hand-held assistive devices for more than two weeks
11. End-stage renal disease requiring chronic dialysis—a completed form CMS 2728-U3 is needed in file
12. ALS, also known as Lou Gehrig's disease

If you or someone you know has one of the conditions described above and meets the other SSI requirements regarding income, resources and U.S. citizenship, SSI presumptive disability or presumptive blindness benefits may be the one of the quickest forms of disability benefits you can receive, even though the payments could stop after six months if no medical decision has been made.

The main requirement that both Social Security and SSI have in common is that the person applying for disability benefits must be unable to perform "substantial gainful work" because of a "severe impairment" that has lasted or can be expected to last at least twelve months or result in death. For 2015, earnings over $1090 a month (or $1820 a month for legally-blind individuals) are generally considered to represent substantial gainful work activity, and are usually sufficient to cause a claim to be denied for either Social Security or SSI if a person is earning that much in the month their application is filed, regardless of the severity of that person's medical conditions.

Aside from Social Security and SSI, there are a variety of disability-related benefits for which you can apply, if you qualify, that are administered by other agencies, such as temporary disability benefits, worker's compensation, long-term disability pensions, Federal, state and municipal pensions for employees of government agencies, and veteran's benefits.

Temporary disability benefits are paid in some states by an employer's insurance company; they can be paid for up to 26 weeks (six months) for an injury or illness which not job-related, unlike worker's compensation benefits which are paid because of a job-related injury or illness. Contact your employer's benefit department or your state's office of worker's compensation to find out how to apply. Long-term disability pensions are available to employees of some firms, usually large corporations that have chosen to provide it as a benefit; contact your employer for that information as well.

Most Federal employees are covered for disability benefits either under the old Civil Service Retirement System (CSRS) or the newer Federal Employee Retirement System (FERS), both of which are administered by the U.S. Office of Personnel Management (OPM) which can be contacted at 1-202-606-1800 or at www.opm.gov. State and municipal employees often have disability coverage from their own employers. Finally, veterans of the U.S. military can receive benefits from the Department of Veterans Affairs (VA) for a service-related injury or illness; they can be reached by calling 1-800-827-1000 or at www.va.gov.

The main thing you need to know about these other disability-related benefits is that many people who could otherwise be receiving a regular monthly income from those programs do not, simply because they are either unaware of those benefits or because they do not understand how to apply. Do not let this happen to you, regardless of the outcome of your Social Security or SSI claim; each agency has its own definition of disability, and most other agencies do not have as strict a definition of disability as Social Security does.

Depending upon which of those other benefits you actually end up receiving, you may have to report those payments to SSA once you have applied for or are receiving Social Security or SSI; they might affect the amount of your monthly SSA or SSI payment or your actual entitlement to benefits. Failure to report this information timely can result in an overpayment of benefits that will usually have to be repaid to SSA.

In the next chapter, I will explain the medical decision process.

Chapter One--How Do You Meet the Medical Requirements for Disability?

When the medical portion of your claim is sent for a decision, the evaluation is done according to what is known as a "sequential" process. This means the information is reviewed in a specific order.

For adult claimants, the first issue to be considered in this sequence is a review of current work activity you are performing, if any. Next comes a review of the severity of your medical conditions, followed by a determination of whether any of your medical conditions meet or equal a "listing" (more about that in a few moments). Finally, an evaluation is made of your remaining ability to perform certain types of activity, which is called "residual functional capacity," as well as a review of your past work, age, education and work experience.

If you found to be either disabled or not disabled at any point in the sequence described, the evaluation ends and the medical decision is made final.

The Listing of Impairments describes impairments in each major system of the human body that are severe enough to make a person medically disabled for the purposes of Social Security or SSI. The "listings" are intended to make it easier for the medical decision-maker to identify those conditions which fit SSA's definition of a disabling condition.

An important point to remember is that although having a medical condition which meets or equals the criteria in the Listing of Impairments is usually sufficient to establish that a person who is not working is disabled, NOT having any of those listed conditions does not automatically mean that a person will not be found disabled; the medical decision-maker is supposed to move on to the next step in the process and apply other rules as described above.

For those of my readers who are interested in seeing the actual listings of impairments along with detailed explanations of how they are used, I will provide a link in the Special Bonus Section near the end of this book.

In the next chapter, I will present the "pros and cons" of hiring an attorney to help you decide whether you need one in your own particular case.

Chapter Two—Do You Need a Lawyer?

When I worked for Social Security, members of the public would frequently ask us whether they needed an attorney for their disability claims. Management made it clear to us in staff meetings that the "appropriate" response to that question was something like the following statement: "You are not REQUIRED to have an attorney; whether you NEED one is up to you (emphasis mine)." While technically correct according to the law and regulations, that statement does not tell you what we inside the agency know about the attorney's role in the disability process.

You have probably seen daytime television commercials advertising the services of law firms who promote themselves as Social Security disability "specialists." Although it is true that such firms usually focus on handling Social Security claims instead of other areas of law such as personal injury or criminal law and they may be more familiar with the disability process than an attorney in a general practice, the practical reality is that they are basically a middleman, especially in an initial claim (before any appeals have been filed).

What this means is that they fill out the same application that SSA employees use in their offices or that you can fill out yourself on the internet, and if your claim is approved the law firm often collects up to 25% of any retroactive benefits that would have otherwise been payable to you AND EVERYONE ELSE eligible on your record, including your spouse and children, up to a limit of $6000.

After they have you sign that type of standard fee agreement and fill in the blanks on the application, they forward the claim to the local Social Security office that you would normally deal with in your area, to be reviewed by the same employees who review claims filed in their own office or on the internet. Frequently the SSA reviewer finds that the law firm failed to provide some piece of required documentation such as a signed medical release form (SSA-827) from the client or proof of legal residency in the U.S., or did not sufficiently explain the client's work history to the extent needed to determine the proper date of onset for the disabling condition.

In cases such as mentioned above, SSA is legally not allowed to contact the client directly if there is a signed Appointment of Representative form in the claim file; they are supposed to contact the attorney's office by mail or phone for the required proof or information and wait until the attorney has contacted the client and obtained what SSA requires. Sometimes SSA has to follow up to the attorney with a second or even a third request, each time allowing several business days for a response. If the attorney does not provide the items requested or provides the wrong evidence, SSA will either deny the application or process it in such a way that the client's benefits will be suspended or reduced even if the claim is medically approved; it then become the client's responsibility to submit the required proof after the claim has been finally approved and processed, otherwise no payments will be issued.

I have seen that type of attorney-caused delay happen more times than you would think, especially when you consider that the attorneys are getting paid for their efforts, but remember that the attorneys are often paid a percentage of the retroactive amount, which could be larger if the final processing of the claim is delayed. I am not saying that attorneys necessarily delay their clients' claims in order to deliberately increase their own fees, but there is not much of an incentive for them to rush since they have nothing to lose, unless they believe the claim will be denied.

After the initial review, SSA forwards the medical portion of the claim to the state Disability Determination Service (DDS) which is an agency of each individual state's Department of Social Services. The DDS requests medical records from the sources listed on the Disability Report, reviews any medical records submitted with the claim, and if necessary schedules a consultative examination with a private medical practice that has a contract to perform such services for them.

Once they have either received the information they requested or determined that they cannot obtain it because the source has failed to respond, the DDS examiner will prepare a written medical decision and make an input to the SSA computer system that will indicate whether the claim has been approved or denied.

As you may have noticed, there is no mention in the previous two paragraphs of any involvement by the attorneys because they are usually involved mainly in the "front end" of initial claims, which occurs before the medical information goes to the state DDS. Law firms might contact SSA if no medical decision has been made for an extended period, often after an inquiry by their client.

If the medical decision is favorable and if there are any retroactive benefits due, even for only one month, the claim is processed and a notice is sent to the claimant explaining that the attorney fee is being withheld from the retroactive benefits due. If the medical decision is unfavorable or partially favorable, a notice is sent advising the claimant that he or she has 60 days to appeal that decision.

If the claimant files an appeal and is later approved, the attorney's fee is withheld after that appeal decision has been processed, and that fee can be considerably larger than on an initial claim because of the additional time and retroactive benefits due, up to a limit of 25% or $6000, whichever is less. If the appeal is a request for a hearing before an Administrative Law Judge, the attorney or a member of their firm will be present with the client at the hearing to represent them before the judge.

Now that you understand how the process works, you can make a better decision about whether to use an attorney or not. If you feel that you can provide the information required, as detailed in the following chapters, and that you can understand the same questions that the attorney would be asking you on behalf of Social Security, you may decide that you want to file at least the initial claim directly with SSA, either online, in person, or by phone. Doing so could save you up to $6000 in attorney's fees from your retroactive benefits.

Even if you decide to file the initial claim without an attorney, you can still decide to hire one later if the initial claim is denied and you want an attorney to represent you at a hearing before a judge; just make sure that the hearing request is filed by the attorney within 60 days of the date on the denial notice you receive from SSA.

However, if you cannot understand or answer the questions on the application and do not wish to have the application completed by a trained SSA employee who will do so at no cost, you may decide to use an attorney.

If you cannot afford to pay the regular attorney fee, there are numerous legal services agencies willing to represent low-income individuals for free or at reduced fees. Contact your local county or state bar association, or look up "free legal services" or "legal service agencies" on the internet and make some phone calls.

You can also contact the National Organization of Social Security Claimant's Representatives (NOSSCR) at 800-431-2804; they informed me that they have 4000 members throughout the U.S., all of whom are either attorneys or authorized representatives approved by SSA to represent claimants. Since I have no personal knowledge of the quality of the services provided by their members, you will have to do your own research when they give you a referral; ask questions like how long that particular member has been representing claimants for Social Security.

In any case, I hope you will read the following chapters before you make a decision about hiring an attorney, at least for the initial claim.

Chapter Three—Before You File

Taking a little time to obtain the necessary documents and information before you are ready to file the application can save a great deal of time and aggravation later, both for yourself and for the interviewer or reviewer of your disability claim. In addition, having information about your medical and work history together in one place will allow SSA to present a more complete and accurate case to the state disability examiner who will make the medical decision on your case.

First we will begin with the non-medical requirements. SSA has to first establish that the person filing for benefits has enough work to qualify for Social Security Disability, unless that person is only applying as a disabled widow or as a childhood disability beneficiary. (The SSA interviewer or reviewer is supposed to screen for possible eligibility for those types of benefits as well.) For regular Social Security Disability, you have to prove both that you have earned enough total credits in your lifetime AND that you have enough recent earnings to qualify.

As proof of recent earnings, you should have W-2 forms or complete self-employed tax returns for at least the last two years in case those earnings have not already been posted to your Social Security earnings record. You should also have at least your most recent pay stub if you had earnings after the most recent W-2 form.

If you have worked at all since the date when you became disabled, even if the work was only part-time, temporary or seasonal, you will need either a printout of your entire payroll record since that date from your employer or all pay stubs issued after you became disabled.

If you are not a U.S. citizen, you will have to prove legal presence in the U.S. (not necessarily as a permanent resident) in order to receive benefits; that means you will have to show SSA an original document from U.S. immigration authorities, or your benefits will be placed in suspense even if you are approved for Social Security Disability.

If you are a U.S. citizen, you may need to provide your original Certificate of Naturalization if SSA does not have your record updated to show that citizenship was already proven.

If you have applied for or received any worker's compensation benefits you will need all award letters since the date you became disabled, showing all the amounts paid and all the dates benefits began, changed or ended. The check stubs from worker's comp do not have enough information to be used as proof, even if you have saved all of them from the beginning, but they can proof helpful if you are unable to obtain the actual award letters.

The Social Security application will also ask about your marriage history and your children, so be prepared with the dates of each marriage and divorce, spouse's maiden name and Social Security Number if you have it, and the full names of any minor children, disabled children age 18 or over, and children aged 18 who are still full time in high school.

For SSI benefits (Supplemental Security Income) you will have to submit information about any income or resources you have had since the month you first contacted SSA to apply for benefits. SSI is calculated on a monthly basis, so you will have to provide a full record showing the amount of each individual payment and the date it was paid to you. Any cash, bank accounts, life insurance policies with a cash value, U.S. Savings Bonds, IRA/401K accounts, vehicles registered in your name and real estate other than the home where you currently reside must be reported and you will be required to provide proof of the value of those resources unless your estimate of their value is high enough to deny your SSI claim.

For both Social Security and SSI, be prepared to provide your checking or savings account number and the name of your bank (if you have a bank account), so that you can be paid through Direct Deposit to your account if your claim is approved. If you do not have a bank account, you will be issued a Direct Express debit card after your claim is processed, and you can use that card to withdraw your benefits in cash at a nearby ATM.

Those are the basic types of non-medical evidence; we will not waste time discussing other types here but just be aware that additional proof may be requested depending on the facts in your own particular situation.

Now we will discuss medical evidence. If you have medical records in your possession, you are strongly encouraged to submit them, either at the time your application is filed or soon afterward. You might be thinking, "Aren't they going to write for those records after they receive my application?" Yes, they will, but the easier you make it for the disability examiner to get the evidence they need, the better your chances of being approved. Why should they wait to receive a convincing piece of medical evidence when you might have it right at home?

If you don't have the medical records and if your doctor or medical center tells you there is a charge for providing you with those records, you can just let the state Disability Determination Service request them after you file.

It is also important that you submit the right type of medical records. The person who decides your claim is an examiner trained in reading medical records. He or she is more interested in seeing actual laboratory test reports showing specific results and numbers than just a brief note from a doctor's office saying that the person is unable to work. The examiners need to make that decision based on whether the person's conditions meet the "listings" as they are called, which are based on federal guidelines for various types of illnesses. They have to justify such a decision in writing based upon what is actually in front of them, not on someone else's opinion. The more specific and detailed the medical record, the better.

Whether or not you have any medical records in your possession, you should make every reasonable effort to obtain not just the exact name, address, phone and fax number of each doctor, hospital, and clinic who has treated or examined you for conditions related to your disabling illness but also the medical record number, clinic card number or admission number for every hospital or clinic you have visited, along with the dates of admission and discharge.

If you have the hospital discharge form or even the hospital wrist band, those will provide the dates of admission and the medical record numbers. If you don't have a record of when you first and last saw each doctor, try to get that information directly from their office, or at least estimate the month and year.

Be prepared to provide the dates of medical tests that you have already had or that are scheduled in the near future, along with the name of each type of test, the name and address of the place where the test was performed, and the name of your doctor or healthcare provider who ordered the test.

As for medications, you should gather together all of your different prescription bottles or obtain a printout from the pharmacy of all the names and dosages of your medications.

Be ready to provide the name, address and phone number of someone else who can be contacted if you are unable to reached, as well as the same type of information for someone other than your doctors who knows about your condition.

Again, I apologize if some of the above suggestions seem obvious to you, but it is precisely because they are so obvious that makes them likely to be overlooked! Trust me, I've seen it happen many, many times.

Chapter Four—Applying Online

The easiest and most efficient way to apply for Social Security Disability is to file online through SSA's website. Even though this method will require more work on your own part in terms of typing on a computer keyboard, it will ensure that the application will be filled out as completely as possible if you take the time to gather and enter all of the information needed to answer all of the questions on the online form. A more complete and accurate application is an application with a better chance of being approved, all else being equal. Even a person with a severe illness or injury can be denied benefits if they do not fill in the right information in the right place or do not provide enough of the right information.

If you are able to successfully complete both the Disability Benefit Application and the Adult Disability Report online, the claims representative who reviews your case at SSA can do so relatively quickly because the computer will alert them to questions that are missing an answer, and after paging through the rest of the application they can decide whether they need to contact you to clarify any of your answers or whether they can transfer your claim immediately to the state Disability Determination Service. Filling out both portions of the online application completely will help your claim get to the DDS as quickly as possible, which means you might receive a decision at least a few days sooner.

Do not complete just the Disability Benefit Application without the Adult Disability Report, because the claim cannot be transferred for a medical decision without medical information; this may seem obvious to you, but people do it all the time. Also, do not complete the Adult Disability Report without the Disability Benefit Application unless you intend to apply in person or by phone.

Once you have gathered all of the information listed in the previous chapter, log on to the internet and to SSA's website at www.socialsecurity.gov. When you get to the home page, click on the top tab that says "Disability," then on the link that says "apply online for disability benefits." Then just follow the instructions listed under "Steps to Apply Online" in the order that they are listed. However, I do suggest that you read the Special Bonus Section near the end of this book before you begin completing the Adult Disability Report—it will help you answer the questions more effectively.

Be sure to use only the "Next" and "Previous" buttons at the top and bottom of each page to move either forward or backward from page to page in the Adult Disability Report, and use the tabs at the top of the page to move between sections. Do not use the "Enter" key or the "Back" button on your browser while you are in the Adult Disability Report.

If you cannot or do not wish to complete the entire Adult Disability Report in one session, you can click the "Sign Off (finish later)" button at the bottom left of any page and then use the Reentry Number which was given to you after you entered your name and address to bring you back to the section where you left during the previous session.

Do not forget to sign form SSA-827, Authorization to Disclose Information to Social Security, because that form is required to give DDS permission to obtain your medical records; failure to submit a signed SSA-827 will delay the medical decision on your claim.

Chapter Five—Applying In Person or By Phone

After reading the previous chapter, if you decide for whatever reasons (lack of internet access, poor typing skills, impaired vision, problems with reading or writing, etc.) that you cannot or do not wish to file for benefits online, you still have the option of coming in to a Social Security Office or applying by telephone. Just realize that once you get to speak to a claims representative, it will usually take them at least an hour (or two) to complete the interview, sometimes longer, depending on how much information needs to be entered for your particular claim; the more doctors, hospitals, medications and tests that need to be listed, the longer your application interview will take. That is why SSA encourages you to come to the interview prepared with the medical information in the proper format to be entered quickly into their computer system.

Even if you intend to file in person or by phone, your interview can be much shorter if you fill out the Adult Disability Report online ahead of time; the interviewer can just import the information you already typed in from the internet and review it, which is quicker than if the interviewer has to type it all in. I would advise you to print out all of the information on the completed Adult Disability Report and bring it with you, just in case the interviewer cannot retrieve it from the internet.

If you cannot fill out even just the Adult Disability Report online, you should go to this link: http://www.socialsecurity.gov/disability/disability_starter_kits_adult_eng.htm and click where it says "Worksheet" to download and print a simple, two-sided form that neatly summarizes most of the basic medical information that the interviewer needs and gives you blank spaces to fill in those facts; I highly recommend that you do at least this much before you apply.

When you have made the decision to apply in person or by phone, you should call immediately to make an appointment, because SSA can use the date you called as the application date, if it makes a difference in the date you are first due benefits; if you delay calling until the following month, you might end up costing yourself and anyone eligible on your record one month's check!

SSA's toll-free number is 1-800-772-1213. They will attempt to give you the earliest available appointment, and you should specify whether you prefer an in-office or telephone interview. Make sure you give them a phone number where you can be reached before the appointment date in case they need to reschedule your appointment for some reason. A telephone appointment is especially useful if it is difficult for you to travel or if you think you will be uncomfortable waiting in a usually crowded reception area and then sitting at an interviewer's desk for at least an hour or more; the phone appointment is for a specific hour on a specific date, and the interviewers do their best to call you as close to that scheduled time as possible.

An in-office interview is useful when you need to bring another person with you to assist you in providing SSA with the information they need for your claim. You can bring someone with you to act as a translator if you do not speak or understand English well, if you need a sign language interpreter, or for any other reason. However, to make sure that the person you bring with you doesn't actually make the interview more difficult, here are a few suggestions based on my experience:

1. Do not bring more than one person with you to the interview unless absolutely necessary.

2. Try not to bring children to the office unless there is no one else to take care of them while you are being interviewed; if necessary, bring someone to sit with the child in the reception area during your interview, but be prepared for them to wait there for you for as long as needed to complete the application process.

3. If you bring someone to assist you as an interpreter, make sure they have a good understanding of both English and your native language; I could write a hilarious skit based on actual interviews I've seen where the so-called "interpreter" either didn't speak English much better than the applicant or didn't speak the foreign language well, or the interpreter was elderly and hard of hearing! Using an interpreter to translate each question and answer makes the interview take about twice as long as usual; using a bad interpreter can make the interview unreasonably long and difficult.

4. In some cases you would be better off to inform SSA at the time the appointment is made that you need an interpreter, and they can use a translation service over the phone during the interview if they do not have an employee available who speaks your language. Many SSA interviewers speak a second language, especially Spanish. For sign-language interpreters, you might have someone contact the local office directly, in advance, so that they can arrange for an interpreting service to assist you.

5. DO NOT bring someone with you to the interview if you think that person is either going to try to dominate the conversation with the interviewer or if they are likely to argue, ask too many unnecessary questions or otherwise interfere with the process. The interviewer has the right to ask the other person to remain silent or even to leave the interviewing area if that person is being disruptive or distracting the interviewer's attention.

6. In the case of an interpreter who is translating for you, that interpreter should be translating exactly what the interviewer says directly to you and vice versa; it is not the interpreter's role to answer in your place, to change your answers, or to tell you how to respond to a question. Again, if the interviewer suspects that the interpreter is doing any of those things mentioned, he or she can tell them to stop doing it and can terminate the interview if they continue to do so. An application for benefits is a serious legal transaction and the interviewer has to ensure that the person applying for benefits is providing correct answers because that person is the one who can be held liable for providing false or misleading information, not the interpreter, and can be subject to penalties based on their own statements.

When you come in for an in-office appointment, make sure you bring an official government-issued photo ID and try to arrive at least 15 minutes before your scheduled appointment time just to provide enough time to "check in," which I will explain shortly. Do not expect to be interviewed earlier than your scheduled appointment time even if you come in much earlier, although it is possible depending upon how many people come in earlier than you, both with and without appointments.

Also, if you check in more than 15 minutes after your scheduled appointment, you will probably be told that you missed your appointment and that you can reschedule for another day; this may seem harsh or overly strict, but SSA has barely enough staffing to deal with the volume of customers it gets each day, and if they let you come in late they might not be able to take the next appointment on time. That would not be fair to the next person who does not come in late, or to people who have already been waiting longer than you without an appointment for other types of interviews.

To check in you will either put in your Social Security number at an electronic kiosk when you walk into the office, take a number from a machine or from a security guard and wait until your number is called to a window in the reception area, or stand in a line until you are called to the next available window. If you enter your SSN at a kiosk, please make sure all the digits are correct, otherwise someone else's name may be called by the interviewer instead of yours when it is your turn and you will not realize they are asking for you! Sometimes people just come in and sit down without checking in, not realizing that they have to inform the office staff that they actually came in for the appointment (we used to get a lot of "no-shows"), then they wonder why no one has called their name. Either way, you might end up sitting in the reception area for a long time because no one realizes that you are there.

Once you check in, do not leave the reception area unless absolutely necessary, and if you must, tell a security guard, give the guard your name and come back as quickly as possible. If your name is called and you do not respond, even if you are standing just outside the entrance, your name will be removed from the list of those waiting to be called and it will be noted that you "left without service," which means you have lost your turn. You snooze, you lose! (I actually have had people tell me they didn't respond to their name because they fell asleep in the reception area. It might have been true, but how were we supposed to know they were there?)

Once you are called in for the interview, please allow the claims rep to do their job! Most are quite experienced at interviewing and know how to obtain all of the information they need in the shortest amount of time. Listen to each question carefully and try to answer as directly and briefly as you can. The most common time-wasters in an interview usually consist of either long, overly-detailed answers to simple questions or answers that do not address the subject of the question directly.

If you do not understand a question, ask the interviewer if they can explain it another way or to give you examples of the type of answers they are looking for. Although you may be justified in asking what the purpose of a particular question is so that you can give a more accurate response, please do not annoy the interviewer by challenging them with "Why do you need to know that?" as if they were asking just to satisfy their own personal curiosity; most questions are either standard interview procedure or are required to fill in the blanks on an application screen.

If any questions arise in your mind either before or during the taking of the application, try to jot them down quickly and wait at least until the application has been printed and handed to you to read before you start asking your questions; this way you do not interrupt the flow of the interview or "derail" your interviewer's train of thought, which only serves to lengthen the interview unnecessarily. You will find that most experienced interviewers will have anticipated many of your questions and answered them by the end of the interview, even if you forget to ask, because certain common questions come up quite frequently and the interviewer has heard them many times before.

At the end of the interview, make sure you put away the receipt for your application, your list of reporting responsibilities (which you should read when you get home) and pick up all of your documents and personal belongings before you leave the interviewer's desk.

Chapter Six—While Your Application is Pending

When you have completed your application and the medical portion of your claim has been transferred to the state Disability Determination Service, they will send a copy of your signed form SSA-827 to each doctor, hospital, clinic and other medical source listed on the Adult Disability Report; this will verify to each source that you have give your permission to release your medical records to DDS for the purpose of making a decision on your claim for disability benefits. Your case will be assigned to a particular disability examiner at DDS, and you will be sent a letter informing you of the name and phone number of that examiner.

You may be sent a questionnaire to complete and mail back if you stated that your medical conditions cause you pain or other symptoms; the DDS examiner needs that information to determine how much your injuries or illnesses affect your ability to function. You might also receive a form asking for more specific details about each type of work you performed in recent years.

If you have any additional medical evidence that was not submitted at the time when your application was filed with Social Security, including new medical information or records from doctors or other providers whom you first visited after filing your application, you can wait until your claim has been assigned to an examiner and contact that person directly by phone, or you can bring it in to the Social Security office and ask them to scan the information into your electronic disability file.

At this point I should caution you about when to contact the DDS examiner. Unlike the claims representatives at Social Security, DDS examiners usually deal with the public only when the examiners need information from individuals who have filed for benefits; their focus is not on answering questions from the public. Therefore, you should not contact the examiner assigned to your case unless he or she is the only person who needs your information or who can tell you why there has still been no medical decision on your claim after four or five months. Medical information from a new source IS a valid reason for contacting the examiner.

Also, if you contact Social Security after your claim has been pending more than four or five months and they verify that no medical decision has yet been made by the state, you can call the examiner and ask if you can assist them in obtaining medical records from any sources which have not yet provided them; in that case, they may actually be glad that you called and tell you exactly which reports they have not received. I have often seen denial notices from DDS which state, "We did not obtain records from any other sources because no others were available." If you can call your doctor's office and get them to respond to the examiner's request, that might make all the difference between being approved and being denied.

After reviewing your statements on the Adult Disability Report, any medical records you have submitted, and reports received directly from the medical sources you listed, the disability examiner may decide to schedule a consultative examination for you with a doctor. This does not happen in every case, but is probably more likely if the medical sources you listed do not include any doctors who specialize in treating your particular type of medical condition, if your medical information does not include enough recent examinations or treatments, or if the DDS examiner wants a specific type of test performed. If you do not list any recent examinations, tests or treatments when you file your application, it is almost guaranteed that you will be sent to such an examination.

There is no charge to you for the visit because the doctor has a contract with SSA to perform the examination on their behalf. The only thing you must do is actually show up for the exam on the scheduled date and time; if you fail to do so, that will be considered a failure to cooperate and your disability claim will be denied, unless you inform the DDS examiner in time that you will be unable to attend for some truly valid reason and the examiner agrees to reschedule for another date.

Over the years, many disability claimants have complained to Social Security after the fact about the quality of their consultative examinations. I have had people at my desk tell me that the doctor who performed the exam rushed them out after a brief conversation, often without doing any meaningful physical examination and usually without performing any standard medical tests.

In recent years, we were told by SSA management that the agency had made efforts to respond to such complaints by reviewing the performance of the doctors contracted to perform the examinations. I have no personal knowledge regarding the extent or effectiveness of such efforts on improving the quality of the examinations; the only advice I can give you is that if you are denied benefits and you truly believe that a shoddy consultative examination was a major reason for being denied, you should state that belief in writing on your appeal request so that the Administrative Law Judge can review the report of that examination in your claims file.

I recall a number of claimants inquiring about the status of their claim after the consultative examination, as much as three weeks afterward, because they had not yet received a decision by that time; in most of those cases the decision had not yet been written and input by the DDS examiner, although sometimes the decision had just been input and the claimant had just not received the letter yet. Based on those instances, I would advise you to wait about 30 days after the examination before you contact the examiner to request status on the decision, and if you do so, verify that the report was received by the examiner before you inquire about how much longer it might take until the final determination is completed.

On its web site, SSA advises disability applicants that most claims take three to five months to process. During my career, 120 days (four months) was about average for most claims, although some could take five months, six months or occasionally even longer.

In recent times certain categories of claims have received an expedited decision: originally those special procedures were applied to cases involving terminal illnesses, and later certain cases began being flagged by SSA's computer system as likely to receive quick disability determinations based on the nature of the illnesses listed. Sometimes those special categories receive a decision within weeks or even days instead of months. Unless you are told otherwise, you should assume that the decision will probably take three to five months.

Some people who apply for disability benefits decide to try going back to work before the medical decision is made on their claim. I should caution you that if you are considering doing that, either because of your own financial need or just because you feel that your medical condition has improved, the DDS will send back your claim without a medical decision to the local Social Security office once they become aware that you have returned to work; your claim will be denied unless SSA has made the decision that the work you are doing is not substantial gainful work.

Even worse, if you go back to work before the medical decision and then inform SSA after your claim has been approved, SSA will have to return the claim to DDS so that they can revise the original decision to a denial, which will result in an overpayment because all benefits paid out already to you will likely have to be repaid. Also keep in mind that some people who return to work find that they are unable to continue working for long and eventually have to reapply for disability.

If you wait to return to work at least one year from the date that you became disabled and begin working after your claim has been fully processed, you will usually qualify for a trial work period, in which you can work and earn an unlimited amount for up to nine months before a decision is made as to whether you are performing substantial gainful work.

In the next two chapters, we will discuss what happens after the medical decision.

Chapter Seven—If Your Claim is Approved

If you have followed all of the suggestions given in this book and your claim is approved, congratulations! You might first receive a letter from the state DDS examiner informing you that the medical decision in your case is fully favorable, and that you will be receiving a separate letter from SSA to confirm that your claim has been processed for payment, known as a "Notice of Award." If SSA requires any additional proof before they begin your payments for Social Security Disability, they will contact you by phone or mail to request that proof, otherwise your claim is often processed automatically after the medical decision is input by DDS.

Hospital and medical insurance under Medicare is available to individuals who have been entitled to Social Security Disability for 24 months (two years). This means that even if you are found disabled prior to the month of application and are paid up to 12 months back in retroactive cash benefits, you will still have to wait at least 12 months from the month of filing for Medicare to begin, unless you are disabled because of Lou Gehrig's disease (ALS) or are on kidney dialysis.

Medicare enrollment is automatic for people receiving Social Security Disability; you do not have to contact Social Security to enroll because you should receive a Medicare card in the mail after you have been entitled to 24 months of disability benefits. Unless you refuse health insurance through Part B of Medicare, Social Security will automatically begin deducting the premium for Part B coverage from your monthly benefits as of the first month you qualify.

You would not usually refuse Part B unless you are currently covered under an employer group health plan as an active employee yourself or as the spouse of an active employee who is currently enrolled in such a plan; if you do refuse Part B, you will be issued a new Medicare card valid only for hospital insurance and will need to reapply for Part B soon after your employer group health plan coverage ends.

If you are medically approved for SSI, no regular monthly payments will begin until after you have been called in for another interview to determine whether there have been any changes in income, resources or living arrangements from what was stated on your application. The local SSA office will usually send you a letter requesting you to come in with specific types of documents to verify the information that you gave them. You must respond to that request and bring in as much of that proof as you can; if you have difficulty obtaining any particular document, contact SSA immediately, preferably at a specific telephone extension if listed on the letter, or come in with all of the other information you do have and you will be instructed as to what needs to be done.

In most states, you may be automatically eligible for Medicaid if you are approved for SSI because the SSI application is also an application for Medicaid, but in some states you must apply separately for Medicaid. Unlike Medicare coverage which usually has a 24-month waiting period, Medicaid coverage generally begins when an individual starts receiving SSI.

If you are entitled to both Medicare and SSI, some states will pay the monthly premium for Part B coverage on your behalf and the amount of that premium will not be deducted from the monthly Social Security benefit once that "state buy-in" goes into effect.

For both Social Security and SSI, if the medical decision states that a representative payee needs to be appointed to handle your benefits, you will need to come in with another person, preferably a relative or a good friend, who is willing to take the responsibility of making sure all of your living expenses are paid on time each month and whom you can trust not to misuse your money. That person will have to bring in their own photo ID and social security number and file an application to become your payee.

Later on, if you feel that your condition has improved to the point where you can handle your own benefits, you can come to Social Security with a letter from a qualified medical professional, preferably a psychologist or psychiatrist, stating when that doctor last examined you and whether you are now capable of handling your own funds. However, even after considering the doctor's opinion, the Social Security Administration has the authority to decide whether a person no longer needs a payee.

Once you begin receiving benefits, you (or your payee) become responsible to report certain changes to SSA. Among the most important changes to report for Social Security Disability are changes in worker's compensation benefits and returning to work. If you begin receiving worker's compensation after you apply for Social Security Disability, you should submit your worker's compensation award letter to SSA as soon as you receive it, because your Social Security benefits might have to be reduced, depending on the amount of the worker's compensation benefit.

If you are receiving worker's compensation when you apply for Social Security Disability, submit any new award letter sent to you showing that the worker's compensation amount has changed or stopped because that might change the amount of your Social Security benefit.

If you return to work, even part-time, temporary or seasonal employment (or self-employment), you need to report that fact promptly to Social Security. The best way to report your work is either by phone or in person at a Social Security office. Either way, make sure to ask the SSA interviewer to provide you with a receipt so that you have proof of the date you reported as well as the facts about your work; this receipt might become very important in case Social Security does not make a timely decision about how your work affects your benefits, because it can be proof that you are not at fault if the work was reported in time to prevent an overpayment but was not processed in time.

Once the report has been processed, you will receive a letter explaining the decision about your work. If you do not receive a decision by four months after the date you make the report, follow up by contacting SSA and have your receipt with you at the time you call or come in.

If you are approved and begin receiving benefits for SSI, you have to promptly report changes in your income, resources or living arrangements. You may be asked to provide proof of the change and proof of the date when it occurred. SSI is based on need and the benefit amount can change from month to month depending on your other income.

SSA is supposed to review the medical condition of an individual receiving Social Security Disability or SSI at least once every seven years, and more often for certain conditions. This means you will receive a short questionnaire in the mail when your case is scheduled for a medical review, which you must complete and mail back. After reviewing the completed questionnaire, SSA may decide to conduct a full medical review and either mail you the forms to fill out at home or send you a letter to come into the office. If you do not respond, or if you do not provide enough useful medical information, your benefits may first be suspended and later terminated completely if the state DDS is unable to conduct a medical review because of your failure to cooperate.

Despite the public perception of Social Security Disability as a "permanent" benefit, all of the changes discussed above can affect the payments you receive. The important thing to remember here is that it is your responsibility to report many of those changes yourself when they occur, not wait until SSA either finds out through other means or asks you about those issues during a future routine interview like a medical review; otherwise, you may have to repay a large overpayment of benefits once Social Security becomes aware of the change.

Similarly, SSA is supposed to conduct regular redetermination interviews after you begin receiving SSI benefits to verify whether any significant changes have occurred in your income, resources, or living arrangements and they can contact you to come in for an unscheduled redetermination if they receive information showing that any of those factors may have changed. These redetermination interviews can result in your having to repay an overpayment unless you can show that you promptly reported such changes at the time they occurred.

Chapter Eight—If You Need to Appeal a Decision

If your claim is denied, or even if is approved as only "partially favorable," which means that you are either found disabled as of a date which is later than what you had claimed on your application or approved for only a "closed period of disability" and are due a one-time payment for a period in the past, you can file an appeal. You will need to look at your denial notice to determine what level of appeal to request; on an initial denial you will be instructed to file either a Request for Reconsideration or a Request for Hearing by an Administrative Law Judge. Either one can be filed online, in person at a local Social Security Office, or through an attorney.

The main difference between these two types of appeals is that a reconsideration request goes back to the state DDS for a decision (by a different examiner than the one who decided the initial claim) or to the Office of Disability Adjudication and Review (formerly known as the Office of Hearings and Appeals), where you have the opportunity to appear before the Administrative Law Judge (ALJ). If your particular state still sends initial denials to the reconsideration level, you will have the chance to request a hearing by an ALJ only after the reconsideration decision.

The most important part of filing an appeal is that it must be done timely. You have sixty days from the date of the initial denial to at least contact SSA and inform them you wish to have them make a notation in their records that you intend to file an appeal; even if you do so, make sure you do not delay filing the actual appeal any longer than is necessary.

If you are unable to contact SSA within 60 days for a valid reason, you should do so as soon as possible and be prepared to submit proof of "good cause" for late filing; if you do not submit such proof, or if it is not accepted as "good cause" by SSA, your appeal request will be dismissed and you will have to file a new initial application, which means you will lose the chance to receive at least some of the retroactive benefits you might have been due from the first application.

During my career as an SSA Claims Representative, I saw many people come back to file a new initial claim after they had failed to come in during the appeals period; when I asked them why they had not filed an appeal, they often stated that they became so discouraged when the initial claim was denied that they had just given up. Some even said that they had torn up the denial letter in disgust, but were coming back to reapply because they could not return to work and had no other income.

Here are some facts that I believe will prove to you that it often pays to file an appeal: according to an annual report by the SSA Office of Retirement and Disability Policy, less than 35% of workers who applied in 2010 and received a medical decision were approved on an initial claim, yet that same report states that 54% of workers were ultimately approved at some level. This means that almost 20% of all initial claims by workers and nearly 30% of all denied initial claims were approved at some level of appeal; those people would never have received disability benefits if they had given up after their initial claim was denied.

Unless you are absolutely certain that you will return to work and be able to continue working after being denied the first time, you should make sure that you file an appeal timely.

To appeal online, go to SSA's website at www.socialsecurity.gov, and on the left side of the home page select "Appeal a disability decision online." On the next page, click on and read "Tips for Using this Website," then close that window and click "Start Your Appeal" on the upper right of the screen. Follow the instructions on each page and make sure that you complete all of the screens that come up.

If you cannot or do not wish to file your appeal online, you can come in to your local Social Security office or appeal through an attorney. If you come in to an office, it is a good idea to complete at least the Appeal Disability Report (form SSA-3441) at home in advance, so that you will save time and have all of your medical information ready to be transcribed by the interviewer. You can obtain the form at this address: http://www.ssa.gov/online/ssa-3441.html.

Whether you file your appeal online or in person, you should have your denial letter from DDS with you and carefully read the personalized explanation of the decision attached behind the cover letter. That explanation follows a standard format: a list of the medical reports used in making the decision, a list of the medical conditions which you claimed on the Adult Disability Report, the findings of the state disability examiner based on the medical reports that were received, and an explanation of why those findings led the examiner to conclude that the evidence shows your condition is not disabling.

On both the Request for Reconsideration and the Request for Hearing, there is a space where you write an explanation of why you disagree with the decision made on your claim. That space is frequently filled in by the claimant with just a short, general statement like "I am too ill to work." A better way is to directly address the reasons for denial given in the denial notice. You can point out which medical sources listed at the time of your application were not considered in making the decision, or that the medical condition stated in the decision is either not the condition you described when you filed or is not the only condition you listed when you applied. You can also challenge the specific findings of the examiner, such as their statements about the amount of pain or physical limitations you have, or the extent to which medication or other treatment has helped improve or stabilize your condition.

The more precise and accurate your statements are in answering the explanations provided with the denial letter, the better the examiner or judge will be able to focus on those issues where the previous decision may have been based on incorrect reading or interpretation of the facts in your case. This makes your appeal request as effective as possible and maximizes your chances for a favorable result.

When you are filling out the Appeal Disability Report, remember to provide only new information that was not given at the time your initial application was filed. You can repeat sources that were listed at the time of initial filing if there have been recent visits for examination, treatment or tests at the same locations after you filed for disability, but definitely list new sources that you first visited after your initial application. List any new medications or tests you have had after you applied, and any new conditions you have developed or that were first diagnosed after you filed.

If any of the original medical problems listed when you first applied have worsened, describe when the change occurred and which symptoms of your original conditions have gotten worse. Do not just repeat the same information listed on the initial claim because that is already in your electronic file.

At the time that you request a hearing before an Administrative Law Judge, you will be asked whether you wish to appear personally at the hearing. Although it is not required to be physically present at the hearing, most people choose to be there because the judge can sometimes tell how your medical conditions affect you just by looking at you, and can ask you questions directly to help determine whether the previous decision was incorrect. Otherwise, the judge will make a decision based solely on a review of the information in the file, checking whether the DDS examiner followed made the correct decision based upon the evidence.

If you have an attorney representing you, the attorney will usually want you to be present even if he or she is speaking on your behalf much of the time.

If you file a reconsideration request and it is denied, you will have 60 days to request a hearing. If a hearing request is denied, you will have another 60 days to file a request for an Appeals Council Review of the ALJ decision; the Appeals Council will review your claim to see if the judge followed proper procedures in reviewing the prior decision. If the Appeals Council disagrees with the ALJ's decision, they can remand the case to the ALJ with instructions to revise the original decision. To request an Appeals Council Review, print out and complete form HA-520-U5, which you can download at http://www.socialsecurity.gov/online/ha-520.pdf, or call SSA to request the form at 800-772-1213, and either mail it to the address shown on the form itself or bring it in to a local Social Security office. You can also obtain and complete the form at your local Social Security office.

If the Appeals Council denies your request, you can still appeal the decision by filing a case against Social Security in a Federal District Court, but you will need to do that through an attorney. Relatively few disability cases are appealed that high up, but I have seen it done and some cases are won at that level.

Once your claim has been denied at a hearing or at the Appeals Council level, you can file a new initial application. However, be aware that the medical decision on the new claim does not have the right to "invade" the judge's decision by finding a person disabled through the date of the latest hearing decision; you may be found disabled as of a date following the latest hearing decision, depending on the medical evidence in your new claim.

In the last chapter, I will provide you with a list of additional tips and suggestions to help guide you as you fill out the different parts of the Adult Disability Report, and explain what type of information the state disability examiner will be looking for in each section.

SPECIAL BONUS SECTION—Expert Tips to Help You Fill Out the Adult Disability Report

The first and most important tip I can give you is to try to imagine that you are the SSA reviewer or DDS examiner looking at your case. Although your particular claim is the only one that matters to you, the person who makes the medical decision sees yours as one of many on a list of cases assigned to him or her for review; they have limited time to spend on any individual claim. Therefore, you want to give that person the most useful information to prove that you are unable to work and to do so in as little space as possible.

As both an interviewer and a reviewer for disability claims, I saw some claimants provide little or no useful information while others would get carried away and write what my co-workers called a "book," giving too much detail; this did not necessarily add much to their chances of being approved and would burden the reviewer and examiner with the task of taking longer than usual to weed through all the excess just to find which answers were relevant to the issues involved in each question.

Therefore, do not repeat information unless it is absolutely necessary in order to answer a particular question, do not provide details related to illnesses or injuries you've had in the past which do not affect your ability to work now, and try to state your main points in one or two sentences rather than lengthy paragraphs. Try to keep your answers clear and simple—you are not applying for the Nobel Prize in literature!

Another general tip may sound obvious, but it can make all the difference in how relevant your answers are: please take the time to read each question carefully, and stop to think before you answer. Try to understand how the question relates to your being unable to work, and provide an answer which makes it clear how your illness or injury has limited you in job-related tasks which you either can no longer perform at all or cannot perform well due to your symptoms.

I will now go through the major sections of the Adult Disability Report one by one so that I can explain the most effective way to fill out each part.

Medical Conditions:

1. List all medical conditions that limit your ability to work. This includes both physical and mental conditions, including emotional problems and learning difficulties, whether they are directly related to your main medical problem or not.
2. Do not list conditions which do not affect your ability to work in any way.
3. If possible, list the exact medical term that provides the official diagnosis for each of your medical problems; you can often find the name of your condition in doctors' letters, medical examination reports, hospital discharge papers, or ask your doctor's office to give you the medical terms for your diagnosed conditions. If you cannot get that information for some reason, be as specific as possible in naming each of your medical problems; for example, "fractured left forearm" is a better answer than "broken arm" and "irregular heartbeat" is more specific than "heart problem."

Please note that the reason it is very important to list ALL conditions limiting your ability to work is that each individual illness or injury you have may not be severe enough on its own to be considered disabling in your case, but the combination of two or more serious medical problems might allow your claim to be approved. This sometimes involves the combination of physical illness or injury with mental illness, emotional problems, or learning disabilities.

Work History:

1. List all types of work you have done in the last fifteen years before you became unable to work due to your illnesses or injuries. Do not list each individual employer; the DDS examiner is only interested in the different job titles you have held and the different skills that were required in each kind of work you did, not how many employers you have had, unless you had to change jobs frequently for reasons related to your illnesses, which you should explain in the Remarks section of the Disability Report.

2. List your official job title and a brief word or phrase that describes each type of employer where you performed that type of work (government agency, non-profit charitable organization, manufacturer, retail clothing store, etc.) For each job title, show the beginning and ending dates of that type of work, the number of hours worked per day and number of days worked per week, the amount of your pay and how often you were paid; estimate the dates or average the amounts if you do not know the exact information, or if the amounts varied over time.

3. If you had only one type of work in the fifteen years before you became disabled, describe your usual duties in that job; list all the major duties as well as minor ones that required extra physical or mental effort. For that job, also write in the number of hours each day you performed various types of physical activity listed on the Disability Report such as walking (from one place to another), standing (mostly in the same area), sitting(including while driving during work hours), climbing (on stairs or ladders), handling large objects (bags of trash, boxes, etc.), writing, typing, handling small objects (like small mechanical parts or hand tools) and reaching (upward, forward or toward your side).

4. Describe what you had to lift at work, about how many feet or yards on average you had to carry it, and about how many times a day you did this in your job. Indicate where required the heaviest weight you ever carried in that job as well as the usual number of pounds you had to lift.

5. If you had to supervise other employees, list the usual number of employees you supervised as well as the amount of your time (either as a percentage of the work day or in number of hours) you spent supervising those employees as opposed to doing just your own work.

6. Indicate whether you were a lead worker, either as a foreman, team leader, or an experienced worker who was expected to train new employees.

7. When asked to list your medications, indicate the name of the medical problem for which each medication is being taken and be sure to list any problems or side effects you have from each medication.

8. In the Remarks section, feel free to write a brief explanation of which symptoms from your medical conditions caused you to stop working and explain which particular tasks required by your job you became unable to perform at all or could no longer perform well enough because of your illnesses or injuries. You can also use that space to explain how any problems you have with reading, writing, speaking or understanding English have made it difficult to do other types of work.

If you read and apply the suggestions given in this section, you will give the examiner who makes the medical decision a clearer picture of the types of work you are qualified to perform as well as how your illnesses or injuries are preventing you from doing those kinds of work. This, in addition to the medical information, will help guide the examiner in making his or her decision. Good luck!

When you are ready to fill out the Adult Disability Report online, you can just use the following link:

https://secure.ssa.gov/apps6z/radr/radr-fe

As promised earlier in this book, here is the link to the Listing of Impairments on the Social Security web site: http://www.socialsecurity.gov/disability/professionals/bluebook/AdultListings.htm You may wish to read the descriptions provided there to see which of those listings might apply to your own medical conditions and also learn what specific information or types of tests the disability examiner will be looking for when they review your medical records. Just click on the general category that fits each of your medical conditions; if you are not sure which ones apply, the following list may help you:

1. Musculoskeletal System—joints, spine, amputations, fractures
2. Special Senses and Speech—vision, hearing and speech
3. Respiratory System--lungs and breathing
4. Cardiovascular System--heart, veins and arteries
5. Digestive System—stomach, intestines, liver
6. Genitourinary Impairments—kidneys
7. Hematological Disorders—blood
8. Skin Disorders—burns
9. Endocrine Disorder—hormone imbalances
10. Congenital Disorders that Affect Multiple Body Systems—non-mosaic Down syndrome
11. Neurological—brain, nervous system, spinal cord
12. Mental Disorders—learning, emotional, substance addiction, autism
13. Malignant Neoplastic Diseases—cancer
14. Immune System Disorders—lupus, scleroderma, connective tissue disease, HIV and other immune deficiency disorders, inflammatory arthritis, Sjogren's syndrome

Conclusion

Now that you have read this entire book, you should have a better understanding of how the application process works for Social Security and SSI Disability. I have given you my best insights based on my training and experience in handling countless applications over the years, and I hope that you will benefit from those insights as much as those people with whom I dealt in person at my desk and over the phone while I was officially an employee of the Social Security Administration.

It is my sincere belief that the ideas and suggestions presented here, while not necessarily unique or earth-shattering, will help reduce some of the anxiety or frustration you may be feeling in dealing with the necessity of applying for government assistance, especially if you have been successfully employed until recently. Just remember that those programs exist for a reason, and that there is no shame in asking for help when you really need it.

Hopefully, some day you might be able to return to work that you find both financially and emotionally rewarding, but until that time you need to pay your bills and have at least enough to survive.

I hope that I have helped make this subject at least a little clearer to you and that you will be able to go through this process more confidently, more relaxed, and better-prepared by knowing what to expect.

Thank you for giving me this opportunity to assist you.

If you have found any part of this book to be particularly useful, I would love to hear about it. Feel free to email me the details of how this book has been helpful to you or someone you know in getting through the application process, as well as any suggestions you might have for other Social Security-related topics that might interest you. Although I cannot guarantee that I will be able to answer every individual question from my readers, I will try to address as many as I can. You can email me at charlesrichfield@outlook.com.

www.ingramcontent.com/pod-product-compliance
Lightning Source LLC
Chambersburg PA
CBHW081412170526
45166CB00010B/3315